SH

Things I Like

I Like Planes

Angela Aylmore

Heinemann
LIBRARY

H www.heinemann.co.uk/library

Visit our website to find out more information about Heinemann Library books.

To order:
☎ Phone 44 (0) 1865 888066
   Send a fax to 44 (0) 1865 314091
📄 Visit the Heinemann Bookshop at www.heinemann.co.uk/library to browse our
💻 catalogue and order online.

First published in Great Britain by Heinemann Library,
Halley Court, Jordan Hill, Oxford OX2 8EJ, part
of Harcourt Education. Heinemann is a registered
trademark of Harcourt Education Ltd.

© Harcourt Education Ltd 2007
The moral right of the proprietor has been asserted.

Editorial: Dan Nunn and Sarah Chappelow
Design: Joanna Hinton-Malivoire
Picture research: Erica Newbery
Production: Duncan Gilbert

Origination: Chroma Graphics (Overseas) Pte. Ltd
Printed and bound in China by South
China Printing Co. Ltd.

10-digit ISBN 0 431 10956 7
13-digit ISBN 978 0 431 10956 5
11 10 09 08 07
10 9 8 7 6 5 4 3 2 1

British Library Cataloguing in Publication Data
Aylmore, Angela
  I like planes. - (Things I like)
  1. Airplanes - Juvenile literature
  I. Title
  629.1'33
A full catalogue record for this book is available from
the British Library.

Acknowledgements
The publishers would like to thank the following for
permission to reproduce photographs: AirTeamImages
2006 Images pp. 7 (Serge Bailleul), 9 (Alex Segre),
17 (Colin Work), 22 (plane at airport, Serge Bailleul);
Alamy pp. 6 (Stock Connection Distribution), 8 (Alex
Segre), 14 (Skyscan Photolibrary), 15 (Purestock), 20–21
(Royan Ong), 22 (biplane, Skyscan Photolibrary); Corbis
pp. 4–5, 10 (Underwood & Underwood), 18 (Tom
& Dee Ann McCarthy), 22 (Wright brothers' plane,
Underwood & Underwood); Getty Images pp. 4–5, 11
(left, Ed Clark/Time Life Pictures), 16 (Eric Cabanis/AFP);
Mary Evans Picture Library p. 11 (right); Photodisc pp.
4–5; Photos.com p. 19; Science Museum pp. 12–13
(Science & Society).

Cover photograph of a plane reproduced with
permission of Getty Images/Johner Images.

Every effort has been made to contact copyright holders
of any material reproduced in this book. Any omissions
will be rectified in subsequent printings if notice is given
to the publishers.

Contents

Some words are shown in bold, like this. You can find out what they mean by looking in the Glossary.

Planes

I like planes.

I will tell you my favourite things about planes.

Flying

I like flying. We go to the **airport** to get on the plane.

I like it at the airport. I watch the planes taking off.

It is exciting getting
on the plane.

I like to sit by a window.
You can look down at the
land below.

The first planes

This is the first plane
that ever flew.

Lots of people tried to make planes. Some of them looked very funny!

You had to flap the wings on this plane! It didn't get very far!

Different planes

My favourite kind of plane is a **biplane**. It has two sets of wings.

This is a **jet** plane. Jet
planes fly very fast.

This is a jumbo jet. Lots of people can fit in this plane.

This is a **microlight** plane.
Only one or two people
can fit in this plane.

Model planes

I like to build model planes.

Some are made from wood.
Some are made from plastic.

This model plane has an **engine**.
It can fly high over the fields.

Do you like planes?

Now you know why I like planes! Do you like planes too?

Glossary

airport place where planes take off and land

biplane plane with two sets of wings

engine machine that makes something move

jet type of engine that is very powerful

microlight type of plane that is very small and light

Find out more

Paper Planes: How to Make and Fly Them, David Mitchell (Collins & Brown, 2006)

Planes, Ian Rohr (A & C Black, 2005)

Planes, K. Khanduri (Usborne Publishing, 2002)

Travel Through Time: Flying High, Jane Shuter (Heinemann Library, 2004)

Index

Titles in the *Things I Like* series include:

Hardback   978 0 4311 0960 2

Hardback   978 0 4311 0957 2

Hardback   978 0 4311 0959 6

Hardback   978 0 4311 0953 4

Hardback   978 0 4311 0958 9

Hardback   978 0 4311 0954 1

Hardback   978 0 4311 0956 5

Hardback   978 0 4311 0955 8

Find out about other titles from Heinemann Library on our website www.heinemann.co.uk/library